stress release information that I have developed or synthesized. There are over three hours of free video training, and nothing is for sale. I am obviously biased, and everyone is different, so what works for one won't necessarily work for everyone. However, I honestly believe this is the best stress release information in the world. If that's not your cup of tea, then that's okay. I will also recommend to you HeartMath, The Work of Byron Katie, or the Sedona Method as what I believe are potentially very effective stress release techniques. Each of these can be learned through a relatively inexpensive book. (I don't recommend purchasing any of the expensive training programs, DVD programs, retreats, or other such things to learn the basics. Your investment should be <$20.)

About the Author

"The secret to happiness is to let go of everything - see through every assumption."

Beginning at a young age Joey Lott experienced intensifying anxiety. For several decades he lived with restrictive eating disorders, obsessions, compulsions, and an inescapable fear. By the time he was 30 years old he was physically sick, emotionally volatile, and mentally obsessed with keeping any and all unwanted thoughts and experiences at bay.

At this time Lott was living on a futon mattress in a tiny cabin in the woods. He was so sick that he could barely move. He was deeply depressed and hopeless. All this despite doing all the "right" things such as years of meditation, yoga, various "perfect" diets, clean air, and pure water.

Just when things were at their most dire, a crack appeared in the conceptual world that had formerly been mistaken for reality. By peering into this crack and underneath all the assumptions that had been unquestioned up to that moment, Lott began a great undoing. The revelation of this undoing is that reality is utterly simple, ever-present, seamless, and indivisible.

Lott's books provide a glimpse into the seamless, simple, and joyous nature of reality, offering a glimpse through the crack in conceptual worlds. Whether writing about the ultimate non-dual nature of reality, eating disorders, stress, disease, or any other subject, he offers the invitation to look at things differently, leaving behind the old, out-grown, painful limitations we have used to bind ourselves in suffering. And then, he welcomes you home to the effortless simplicity of yourself as you are.

Not sure where to begin? Pick up a copy of Lott's most popular book, *You're Trying Too Hard*, which strips away all the concepts that keep us searching for a greater, more spiritual, more peaceful life or self.

Printed in Great Britain
by Amazon

Step 1.
Introduction

Becoming a first-rate artist calls for creativity, staying power and practice. These conduct can flourish in youngsters after they begin to increase them at a younger age. We consider our manual will train your infant the field and staying power required to now no longer simply learn how to draw well, however to apply the ones features in the whole thing they do. Your activity as a determine is to paintings together along with your infant and inspire them whilst caught and experience like giving up.

The global of artwork is an remarkable manner for you and your infant to talk and bond. When you open this ee-e book and begin to create together along with your little one, you may pleasure withinside the stuff you find out about them and they'll experience in the direction of you. Your aid and mild guidelines will assist them be greater affected person with themselves and shortly they'll take some time had to create brilliant drawings of which you could each be proud.

This manual is beneficial for mother and father because it teaches basics of drawing and easy techniques. By following this ee-e book together along with your infant, adults will analyze staying power and increase their talents as a infant's maximum crucial teacher. By spending some hours collectively you may increase a sturdy connection and analyze the fine approaches of speaking with every different. It is actually a worthwhile revel in while you and your infant create a masterpiece with the aid of using running collectively!

Step 2.

How to draw a steam locomotive.

Step 3.

Start with a huge cylinder withinside the middle of the page. Add a deformed triangular form to the the front. Add rectangles to the lowest and upload a dice to the rear.

Step 4.

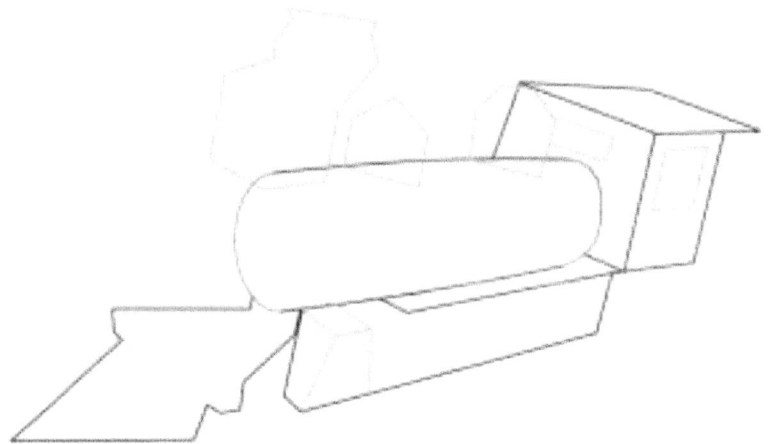

Add the define of the chimneys to the pinnacle of the cylinder. Add the 2 rectangles to the the front and upload the rectangular and rectangle to the dice.

Step 5.

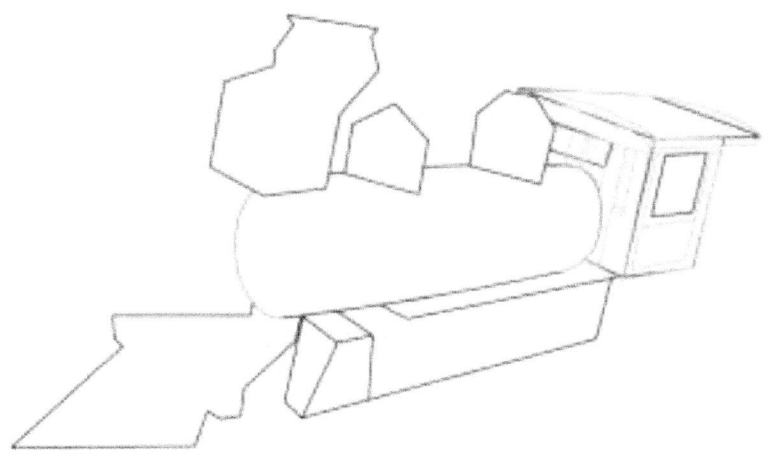

Redraw the dice to provide it a roof. This will function the driver's cabin. Use the rectangular to make the door and the rectangle to make the centerpiece of the window. Add a smaller window proper subsequent to it.

Step 6.

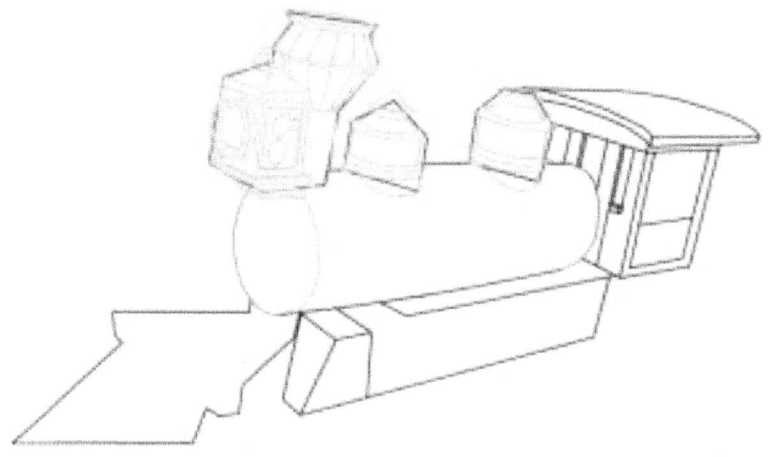

Let's end the ones chimneys! At the the front sits the brilliant mild the teach makes use of to peer beforehand of it. I made mine barely futuristic with the aid of using including some more traces to the lamp itself. On the aspect circles and smaller buttons deliver it a greater mechanical experience. The kettle of the primary chimney curves outward and inward like a vase. The 2d chimney has a small triangle on pinnacle of it, at the same time as the nearly equal 1/3 chimney exposes the hollow on the pinnacle.

Step 7.

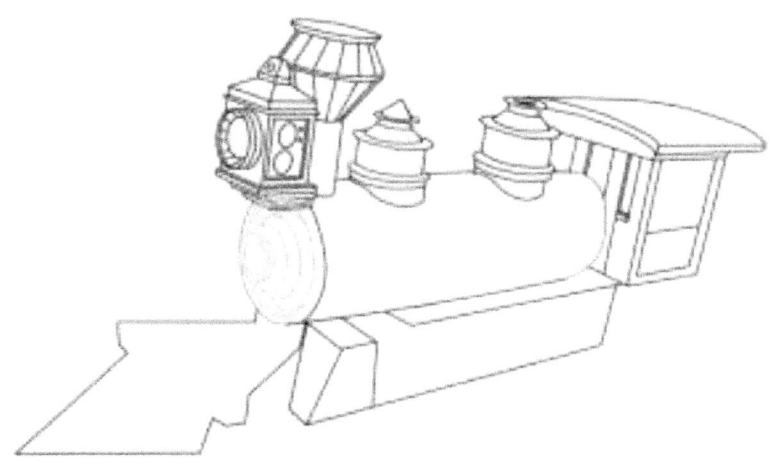

Continue with the the front of the cylinder. As I made mine futuristic in nature, the cylinder bends inwards, with a 3 layered 2d mild sticking out. Ingenious, huh?

Step 8.

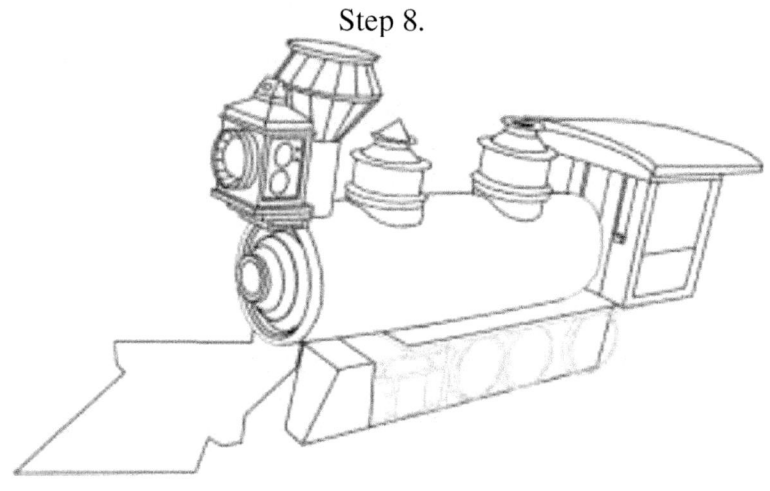

Add a fixed of 3 wheels to the aspect of the locomotive. Add a part of the body proper in the front of it.

Step 9.

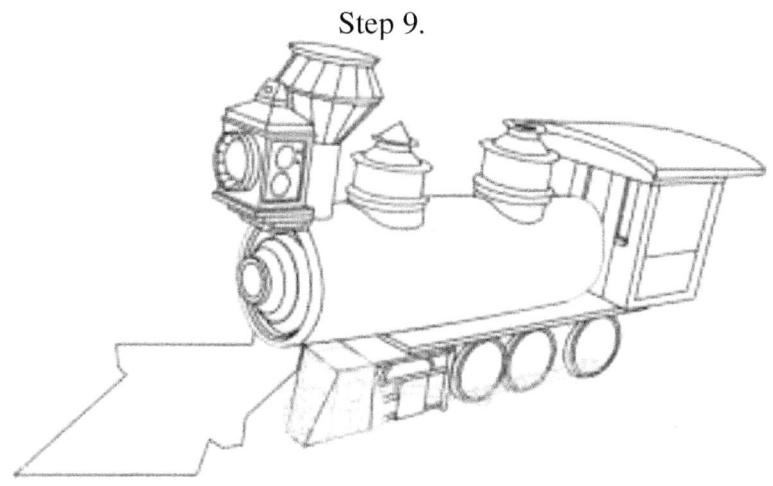

Use the closing the front define to attract the generator and pistons for the metallic bars to propel the wheels. This is probably tricky, so ensure to appearance carefully at the instance that will help you alongside. A dice with a circle up pinnacle, with a cylinder proper beneathneath it. The metallic bars attain out from in the back of it, connected to every different with the aid of using a small dice.

Step 10.

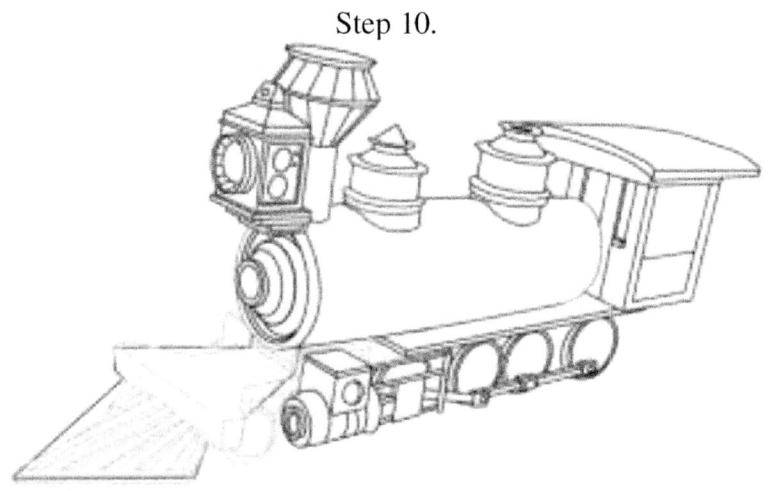

The form up the front we can used to create the snow shovel. It is triangular in nature, connected to an anvil-fashioned platform connecting it to the teach. Then upload what's seen of the generator on the alternative aspect of the teach. Make certain to feature a few aid bars withinside the internal of the teach. Make certain to apply the instance on your heart's desire.

Step 11.

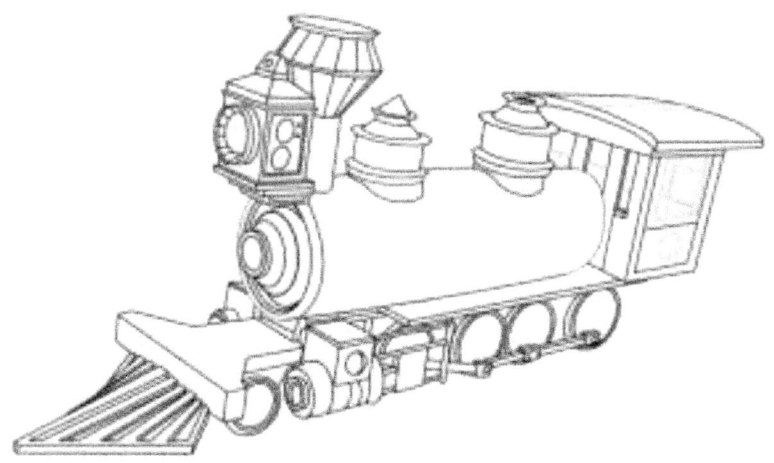

Let's keep with the cabin. Add a circle to the door. Then upload the window body withinside the door with a smaller window at the lower back wall of the cabin.

Step 12.

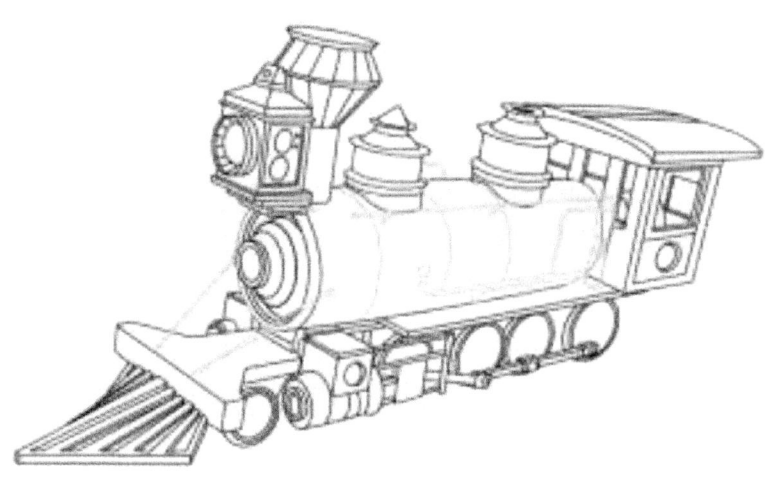

For more aid, upload metallic bars attaining from the platform to the cylinder of the teach. Alongside the cylinder runs a metallic bar connected to the equipment internal, in addition to a bar on the pinnacle of the cylinder. Underneath it runs a pipe related to a steam piston, proper in the front of the cabin. See how the pipe splits into separate traces?

Step 13.

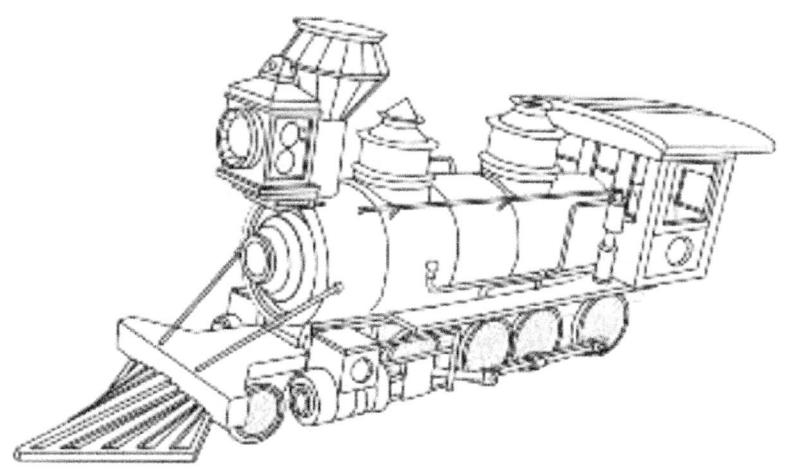

Add the internal of the wheels. A locomotive's wheels have thins spikes jogging from a round middle factor to the outer edges of the wheel.

Step 14.

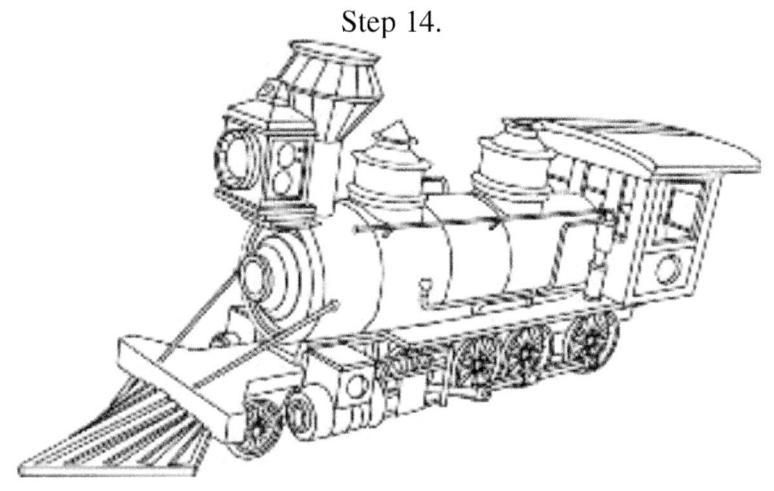

All done! Let's color!

Step 15.

Color yours but you want! I gave the cabin a inexperienced and brown appearance with gold and blue for the details. The main components of the teach are darkish and mild grey. I used pink for the wheels. For the element I used golden yellow, with natural yellow for the lights.

Step 16.

Add a few shadow to deliver it even greater to life.

Step 17.

Colored version.

Step 18.

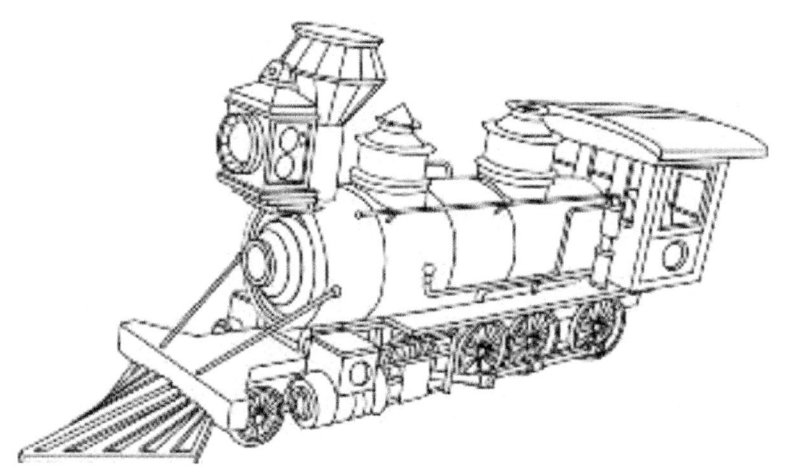

Line artwork.
How to draw a Diesel train.

Step 19.

Step 20.

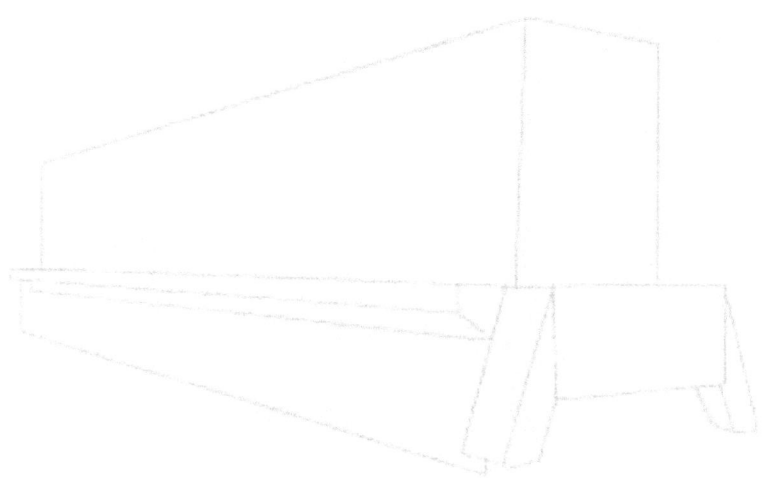

Add a huge rectangle to the middle of your page. Add the M form to the the front. Then upload the rectangles alongside the period of the preceding one to the lowest.

Step 21.

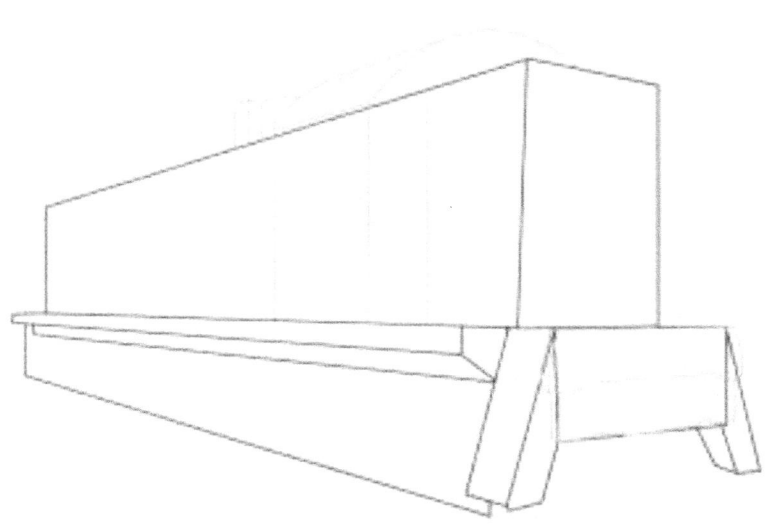

Add 3 traces to the facet of the educate with a curved rooftop above it. Add the vent proper at the back of it. To the the front of the educate, upload plates as withinside the example.

Step 22.

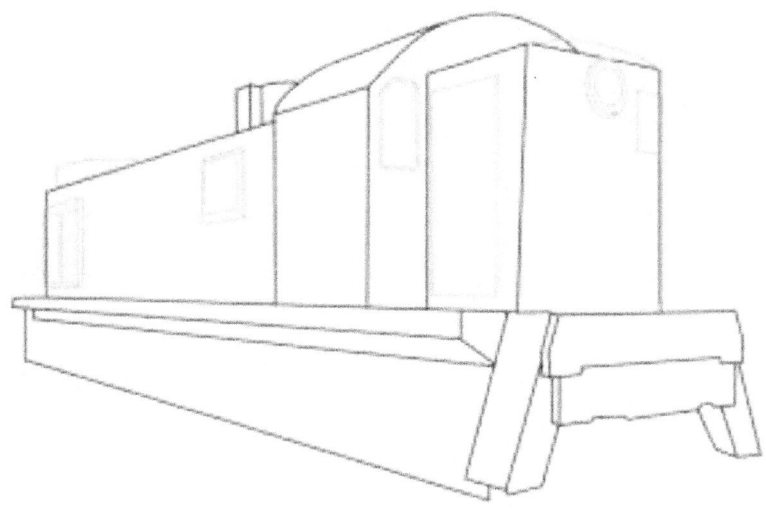

Let's upload a window to the small wall affront the educate. Add a big vent behind the educate with a smaller withinside the middle. Add a brand new form to the returned atop the educate. Now draw a rectangle to the left facet of the the front. Curve pinnacle of the the front and upload a round form under it for the mild. Then upload a small rectangle proper subsequent to it.

Step 23.

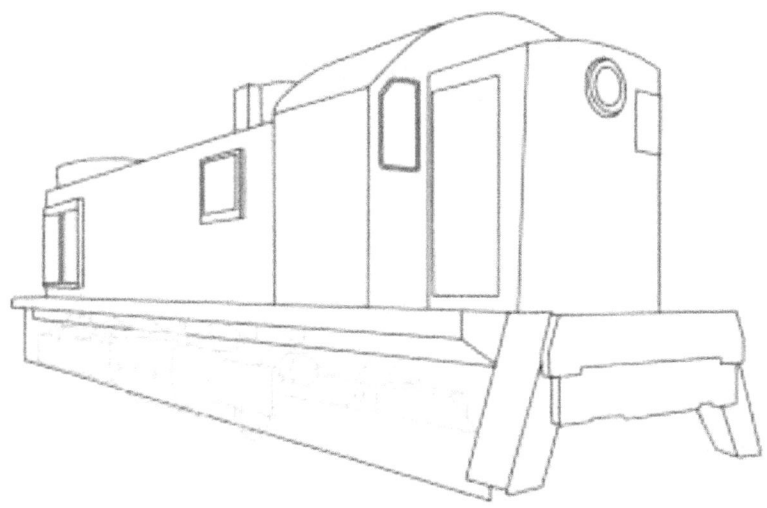

Now we can paintings on the principle a part of the gadget that drives the wheels round. In the middle of the educate is the generator, offering electricity to the mechanism to force the wheels. Attached to it's miles the body. This includes heave steel bars walking from the returned to the the front. Several cylinders assist deliver the electricity even as triangular shapes assist assist the steel structure.

Step 24.

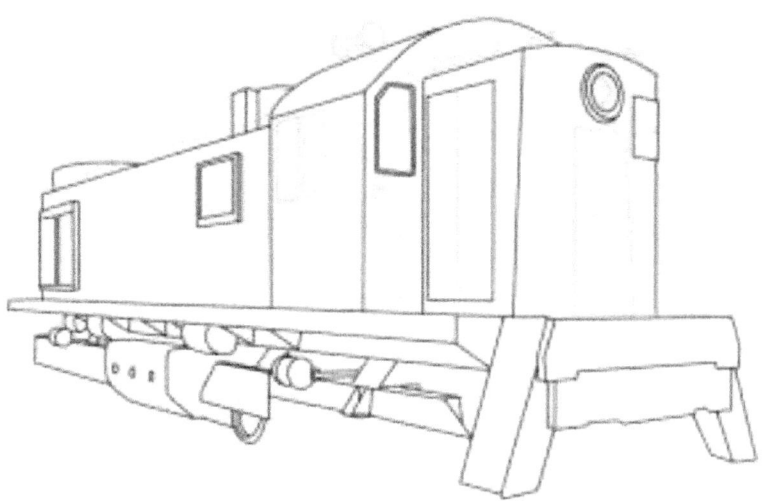

Add a 2d set or square home windows to the facet. Then upload the horn on pinnacle of the educate as withinside the example. Alongside the rims of the educate run a chain of steel bars. These are protection railings for employees to keep on to. Add a 2d line in the the front mild and upload a square form below it.

Step 25.

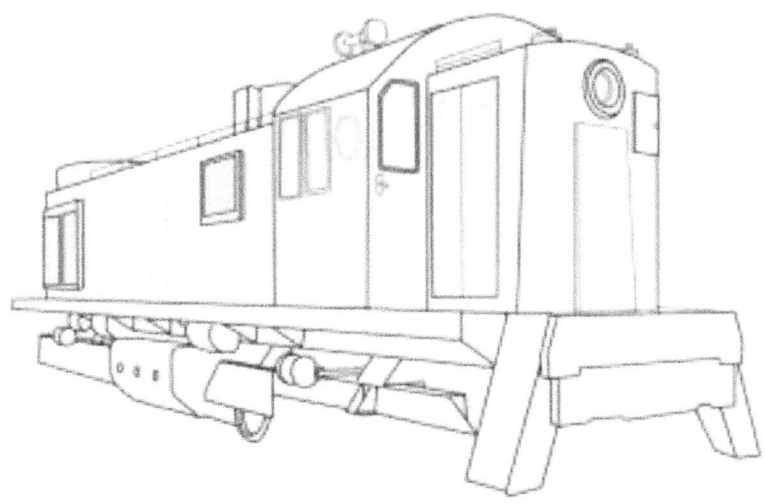

Add a small round window subsequent to the square window. Add horizontal traces internal every of the vents at the facet. Lastly, upload a fixed of 4 rectangles subsequent to the vents.

Step 26.

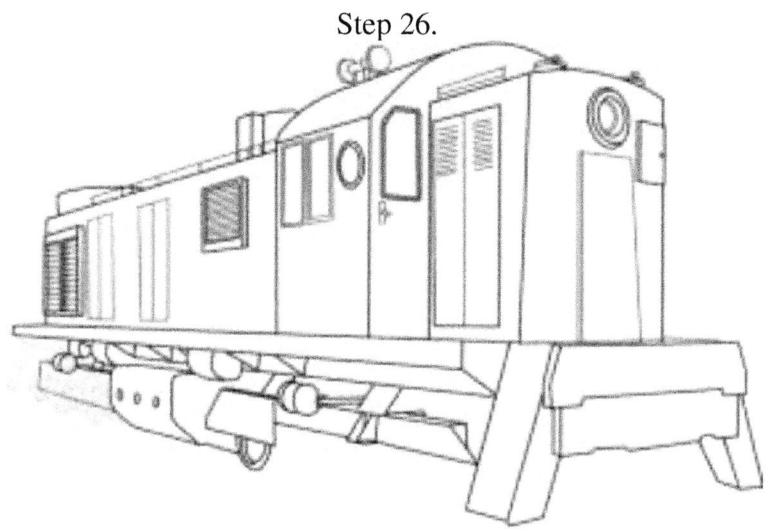

Add a steel plate to the rear of the educate. Now we can begin including withinside the wheels. The wheels are held in region through a big round bolt. The bolt is hooked up to an arched steel bar. Hydraulic cylinders subsequent to the wheels assist the whole gadget. The wheels are lodged at the back of the steel arches, nearly hidden from sight.

Step 27.

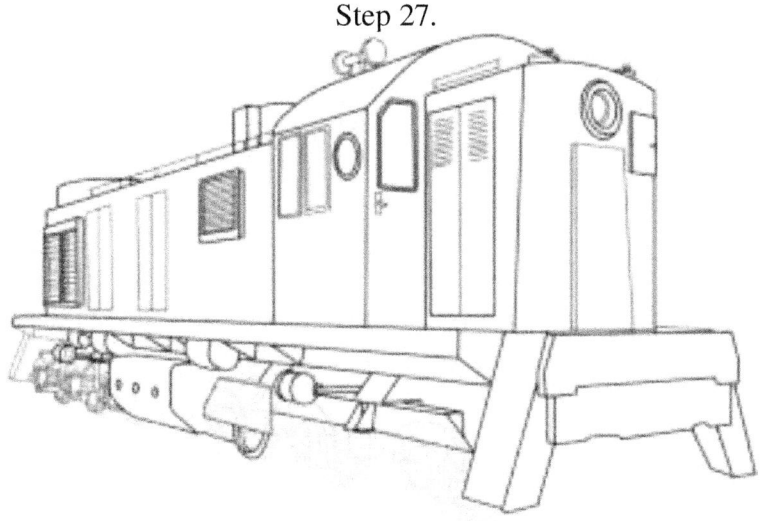

Now do the equal for the the front wheels.

Step 28.

Add a few steps to the the front to assist the motive force climb up the educate. Add the snow shovel to the the front. The educate has a further set of 4 lighting fixtures above the snow shovel. Add the hand below the lighting fixtures to make certain it is able to hook up with different trains if necessary.

Step 29.

Add huge steel railings alongside the edges of the educate to maintain the educate people effectively at the educate.

Step 30.

All done! Let's color!

Step 31.

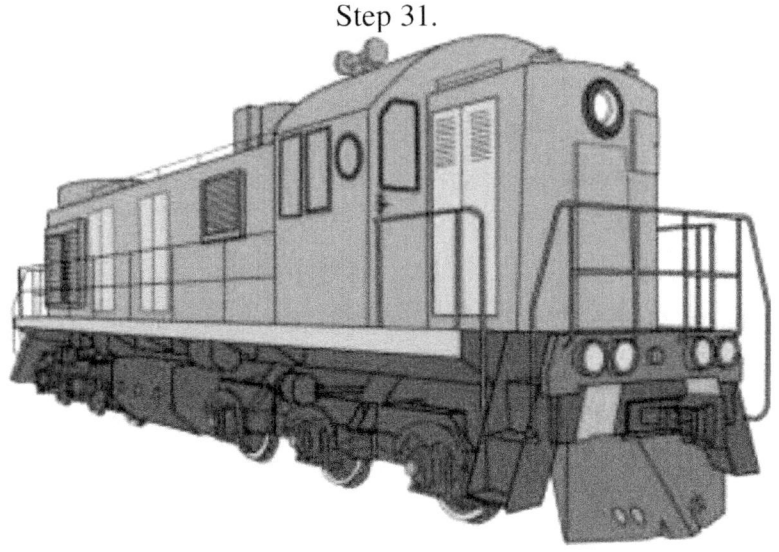

The top a part of the educate is orange, with the lowest darkish gray. The steel bar and the snow shovel I coloured pink, with yellow for details. The majority of the last doors, vents and horn is mild gray. The home windows are a lighter gray.

Step 32.

Add a few shadow to offer it greater life.

Step 33.

Colored version.

Step 34.

Line art.
How to draw a high speed train.

Step 35.

Step 36.

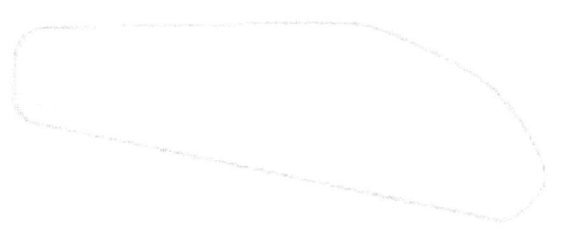

Add a cylinder kind form withinside the middle of your page.

Step 37.

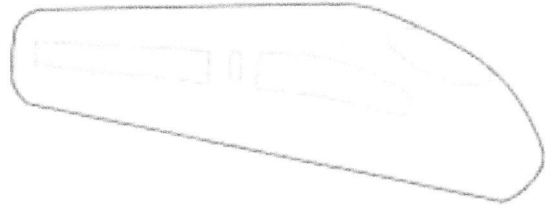

Add 1/2 of a circle for the the front and rectangles following the form of the educate for the home windows.

Step 38.

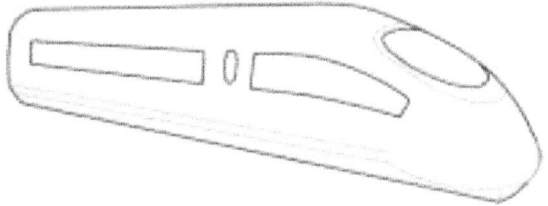

Add window body across the the front window. Then upload the primary directly line down the lowest, with a 2d one following below it curving right all the way down to clean out the the front of the educate.

Step 39.

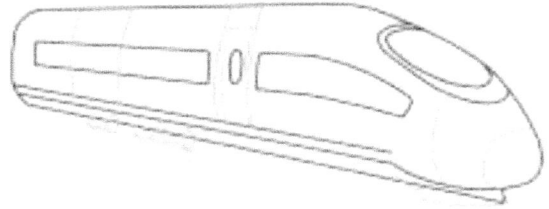

Add a nostril to the the front and a further line round it. Add a door to the facet of the educate, with more traces barely at the back of it, that you fill with more traces at the internal. Add a snow shovel to the lowest on the the front. The excessive pace educate is propelled through the electricity of magnets. On the facet of the educate, upload 3 cubes dealing with down, as though they're pushing the educate off of the ground.

Step 40.

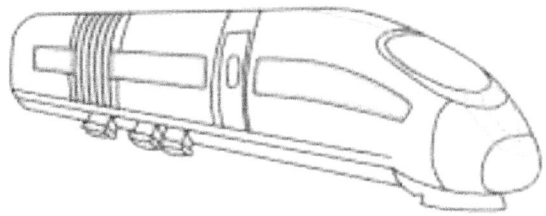

Add a window body in the home windows. Then upload a few sticker to the educate. I selected to feature a few symbols to the the front of the educate.

Step 41.

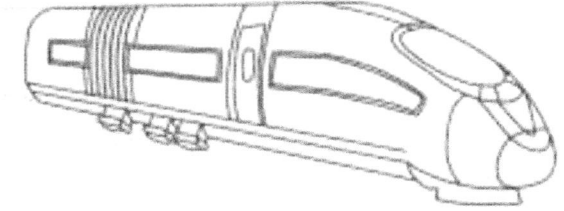

Let's deliver it a coupe. Add 2d rectangle to the returned of the educate.

Step 42.

Add a brand new window internal of it, with greater vertical traces at the back of it.

Step 43.

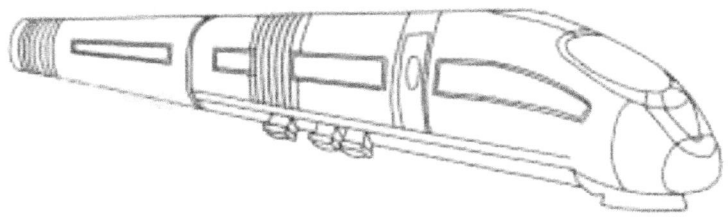

Add greater cubes down the lowest which push the educate off the tracks.

Step 44.

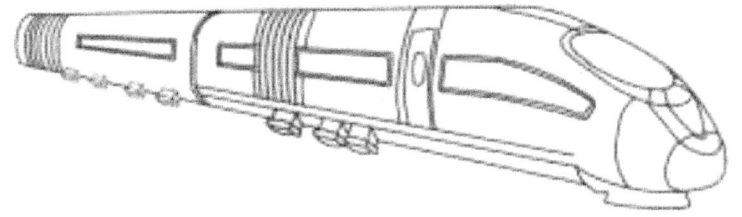

All done! Let's color!

Step 45.

I made mine inexperienced with pink for the symbols. The separate elements are mild gray. The cubes are darkish gray with blue for the magnetic electricity. The internal of the home windows I made darkish inexperienced.

Step 46.

Give it come shadow to deliver it to life!

Step 47.

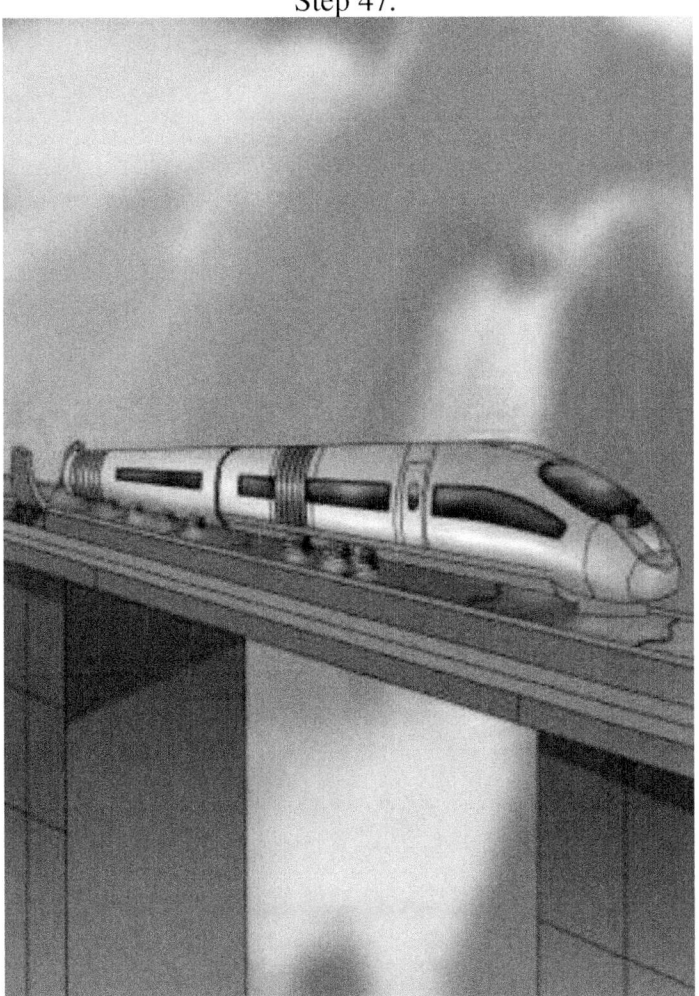

Colored version.

Step 48.

Line art.

Printed in Great Britain
by Amazon